OXFORD

Secular

BC 208

SATB double choir
unaccompanied

CW01582998

Bob Chilcott

SILVER SWAN

The silver swan, who living had no note,
When death approached unlocked her silent throat;
Leaning her breast against the reedy shore,
Thus sung her first and last, and sung no more:
Farewell, all joys;
O death, come close mine eyes;
More geese than swans now live, more fools than wise.

Anon.

Multas per gentes et multa per aequora vectus
advenio has miseras, frater, ad inferias,
ut te postremo donarem munere mortis
et mutam nequiquam alloquerer cinerem,
quandoquidem fortuna mihi tete abstulit ipsum,
heu miser indigne frater adempte mihi.
Nunc tamen interea haec prisco quae more parentum
tradita sunt tristi munere ad inferias
accipe fraterno multum manantia fletu,
atque in perpetuum, frater, ave atque vale.

Travelling through many nations and through many seas
I have come, brother, for these poor funeral rites,
That I might render you the last dues of the dead
And vainly comfort your dumb ashes,
Because Fortune has robbed me of your self, alas,
Poor brother, unfairly taken from me.
But now, meanwhile, accept these gifts which by old custom
Of the ancestors are offered in sad duty
At funeral rites, gifts drenched in a brother's tears,
And forever, brother, greetings and farewell.

Gaius Valerius Catullus (*c.*84–*c.*54 BC)
trans. Guy Lee

Extracts from *The Poems of Catullus*, Translated with Introduction and Notes by Guy Lee (OWC, 1990) pp. 139–41. By permission of Oxford University Press.

Commissioned for the Saint Louis Chamber Chorus, Artistic Director Philip Barnes,
by Matthew Chapman and Leslie Chapman Bell, in loving memory of their brother, Michael Chapman,
and in honour of their parents, Edward and Barbara Chapman.

Silver swan

English text by Anon.
Latin text by Gaius Valerius Catullus (*c*.84–*c*.54 BC)

BOB CHILCOTT
(after Orlando Gibbons)

Duration: 5 mins

Printed in Great Britain

OXFORD UNIVERSITY PRESS, MUSIC DEPARTMENT, GREAT CLARENDON STREET, OXFORD OX2 6DP

5
mp
- ver, sil - ver, sil - ver swan. Sil - ver
mp
- ver, sil - ver, sil - ver swan. Sil - ver
mp
- ver, sil - ver, sil - ver swan. Sil - ver
mp
- ver, sil - ver swan. Sil - ver
mp
The sil - ver swan, who liv - ing had no note,
mp
The sil - ver swan, who liv - ing had no note,
mp
The sil - ver swan, who liv - ing had no note,
The sil - ver swan,

9
SOPRANO SOLO
mp
ah
CHOIR 1
S.
swan, When death ap - proached un -
A.
swan, When death, when death ap - proached, ap - proached un -
T.
swan, When death, when death ap - proached, ap - proached un -
B.
swan, When death, when death ap - proached un -
CHOIR 2
S.
sil - ver, sil - ver, sil - ver, sil - ver swan.
A.
sil - ver, sil - ver, sil - ver swan.
T.
sil - ver, sil - ver, sil - ver, sil - ver swan.
B.
mp
sil - ver, sil - ver, sil - ver swan.

12
p
ah
-locked her si - lent throat;
Sil - ver, sil - ver swan,
-locked her si - lent throat;
Sil - ver, sil - ver swan,
-locked her si - lent throat;
Sil - ver, sil - ver swan,
-locked her si - lent throat;
Sil - ver, sil - ver swan,
Sil - ver swan,
sil - ver
Sil - ver swan,
sil - ver
Sil - ver swan,
sil - ver
Sil - ver swan,
sil - ver

16
mf
ah
mp mf
sil - ver, sil - ver, sil - ver swan. Lean - ing her breast, sil - ver,
mp mf
sil - ver, sil - ver swan. Lean - ing her breast, sil - ver,
mp mf
sil - ver, sil - ver, sil - ver swan. Lean - ing her breast, sil - ver,
mp mf
sil - ver, sil - ver swan. Lean - ing her breast, sil - ver,
mp mf
swan. Lean - ing her breast a - gainst the reed - y
mp mf
swan. Lean - ing her breast a - gainst the reed - y
mp mf
swan. Lean - ing her breast a - gainst the reed - y
mp mf
swan. Lean - ing her breast a - gainst the reed - y

20
sil - ver swan, Thus sung her last, and sung:
sil - ver swan, Sung her first and last, and sung:
sil - ver swan, Thus sung her first and last, and sung:
sil - ver swan, Sung her first and last, and sung:
shore, Thus sung her first and last, and sung no
shore, Thus sung her first and last, and sung no
shore, Thus sung her first and last, and sung no
shore, Thus sung her first and last, and sung no

24
p
ah ah
p
Fare-well, fare - well, fare-well, fare - well, fare-
p
Fare - well, fare - well, fare-
p
Fare - well, fare - well, fare-
p
Fare-well, fare - well, fare-well, fare - well, fare-
p
more: Fare - well, fare-well, fare - well, fare-well, fare - well.
p
more: Fare - well, fare - well, fare - well.
p
more: Fare - well, fare-well, fare - well, fare - well.
p
more: Fare - well, fare - well, fare-well, fare - well,

28
- well, fare - well, fare - well,
mp espress.
- well. Mul - tas per gen - tes et mul - ta per ae - quo - ra vec - tus ad - ve - ni' has
- well, -well, fare - well,
mp espress.
- well. Mul - tas per gen - tes et mul - ta per ae - quo - ra vec - tus ad - ve - ni' has
The sil - ver swan, who liv - ing had no
The sil - ver swan, who liv - ing had no
The sil - ver swan, who liv - ing had no
fare - well, fare - well,

31
CHOIR 1
S.
fare - well, fare - well. When death ap - proached
A.
mi - se - ras, fra - ter, ad in - fe - ri - as. When death, when death ap -
T.
fare - - well. When death, when death ap -
B.
mi - se - ras, fra - ter, ad in - fe - ri - as. Fare - well, fare - well When
CHOIR 2
S.
note, fare - well, fare - well, fare - well, fare - well fare -
A.
mp espress.
note, fare - well. Ut te pos - tre - mo do - na - rem
T.
note, fare - well, fare - well, fare - well fare -
B.
mp espress.
fare - well, fare - well, fare - well. Ut te pos - tre - mo do - na - rem

34
— un - locked her si - lent throat.
- proached, ap - proached un - locked her si - lent throat.
- proached, ap - proached un - locked her si - lent throat.
death ap - proached un - locked her si - lent throat.
- well. Fare-well, fare -
mu - ne - re mor-tis et mu-tam ne - qui-quam al - lo - que-rer ci - ne - rem. Fare-well, fare -
- well. Fare-well, fare -
mu - ne - re mor-tis et mu-tam ne - qui-quam al - lo - que-rer ci - ne - rem. Fare-well, fare-,

37
Fare-well, fare - well. Heu mi-ser
Quan-do-qui-dem for-tu-na mi-hi tet' ab-stu-lit ip-sum. Fare -
Fare-well, fare - well. Heu mi-ser
Quan-do-qui-dem for-tu-na mi-hi tet' ab-stu-lit ip-sum. Fare -
- well, fare-well, fare - well, fare-well, fare - well.
- well, fare-, fare - well, fare-, fare - well.
- well, fare-well, fare - well, fare-, fare - well.
fare - well, fare - - well, fare-, fare - well.

40
mf
in-di-gne fra-ter a-demp-te mi- hi. Nunc ta-men in-te- re' haec pris - co quae mo-re pa-ren- tum
mp cresc.
mf
- well, fare - well. Lean - ing her breast. Pris - co quae mo-re pa-ren- tum
mf
in-di-gne fra-ter a-demp-te mi- hi. Nunc ta-men in-te- re' haec pris - co quae mo-re pa-ren- tum
mp cresc.
mf
- well. Lean - ing her breast. Pris - co quae mo-re pa-ren- tum
mp cresc.
Lean - ing her breast a - gainst the reed - y
mp cresc.
Lean - ing her breast, her breast a - gainst the reed - y
mp cresc.
Lean - ing her breast, her breast a - gainst the reed - y
mp cresc.
Lean - ing her breast a - gainst the reed - y

43
f
tra-di-ta sunt tris - ti mu-ne-r'ad in-fe-ri-as,
f
tra-di-ta sunt tris - ti mu-ne-r'ad in - fe - ri - as,
f
tra-di-ta sunt tris - ti mu-ne-r'ad in-fe-ri-as,
f
tra-di-ta sunt tris - ti mu-ne-r'ad in - fe - ri - as,
f
shore, Thus sung her first and last, and
f
shore, Thus sung her first and last, and
f
shore, Thus sung her first and last, and
f
shore, Thus sung her first and last, and

46
p
dolce
ad in - fe - ri - as. Fare - well, fare - well, fare - well. Fare - well, all
p
dolce
ad in - fe - ri - as. Fare - well, fare - well. Fare - well, all
p
dolce
ad in - fe - ri - as. Fare - well, fare - well, fare - well. Fare - well, all
p
dolce
ad in - fe - ri - as. Fare - well, fare-, fare - well. Fare - well, all
p dolce
sung no more: Fare-well, fare - well, fare - well, fare - well. Fare -
p dolce
mp
sung no more: Fare - well. A - cci - pe fra - ter - no
p dolce
sung no more: Fare - well, fare - well, fare - well. Fare -
p dolce
mp
sung no more: Fare-well, fare - well. A - cci - pe fra - ter - no

50
mp dolce
joys; O death, come close mine eyes; More geese than swans now
joys, all joys; O death, come close mine eyes; More geese than swans now
joys, all joys; O death, come close_ mine eyes; More geese than swans now
joys; O death, come close mine eyes; More geese than swans now
mf dim.
- well, all joys. At - qu'in per-pe-tu-um, fra-ter, av' at - que va-
mul-tum ma-nan-ti-a fle-tu, at - qu'in per - pe-tu-um, fra-ter, av' at - que va-
- well, all joys. At-qu'in per-pe-tu - um, fra-ter, av' at - que va-
mul-tum ma-nan-ti - a fle-tu, at - qu'in per - pe-tu-um, fra-ter, av' at - que va-

54
p
live, more fools than wise. Va-le, va-le, va-
p
live, more fools than wise. Va-le, va-le, va-
p
live, more fools than wise. Va-le, va-le, va-
p
live, more fools than wise. Va-le, va-le, va-
p
-le, av' at-que va-le. Fare-well, fare-well,
p
-le, av' at-que va-le. Fare-well, fare-well,
p
-le, av' at-que va-le. Fare-well, fare-well,
p
-le, av' at-que va-le. Fare-well, fare-well,

58
pp
-le, va-le, va-le, va - le, va-le, va-le, va - le,
pp
-le, va-le, va-le, va - le, va-le, va-le, va - le,
pp
-le, va-le, va-le, va - le, va-le, va-le, va - le,
pp
-le, va-le, va-le, va - le, va-le, va-le, va - le,
pp
fare-well, fare - well, fare-well, fare - well, fare-well, fare -
pp
fare-well, fare - well, fare-well, fare - well, fare-well, fare -
pp
fare-well, fare - well, fare-well, fare - well, fare-well, fare -
pp
fare-well, fare - well, fare-well, fare - well, fare-well, fare -

ISBN 978-0-19-341903-2

Processed in England by Enigma Music Production Services, Amersham, Bucks.
Printed in England by Halstan & Co. Ltd, Amersham, Bucks.